ABOUT THIS BOOK

In *You Got This, Kid! Words of Advice for Young Leaders*, Chuck Saia uses his 30 years of business experience to offer young leaders words of advice through seven unforgettable stories derived from the lives of animals. "You would be amazed at the similarities between the business world and the animal kingdom," Saia says. Analogies between the corporate environment and behaviors found in Mandarin Ducks, armadillos, scorpions, among others, connect with the reader on a personal level. He believes these tales will better serve a reader's memory than what's described in your typical book about leadership.

Saia's direct and down to earth writing style makes for quick reading, inviting most young leaders to sail through the seven short chapters in one sitting.

You Got This, Kid! Words of Advice for Young Leaders, offers a number of life lessons. One asserts that while climbing the career ladder seems to be all about the individual, it's also *not* all about any one person. We learn about teamwork from a number of species. They teach us how each member plays a role in shaping another's future as a leader.

All proceeds from *You Got This, Kid! Words of Advice for Young Leaders,* will be donated for Lupus and Environmental Sustainability research.

YOU GOT THIS, KID!

WORDS OF ADVICE FOR YOUNG LEADERS

CHUCK SAIA, MBA, CPA

Illustrations by
ALEXIA PAPAVASILAKIS

To my mentee's, watching you grow is a gift. To my mentors, thank you.

CONTENTS

NAVIGATING
TREACHEROUS WATERS

"You got this, kid."

My father's voice carried over the sound of rushing water on a hot July day, circa 1981. After many, many seasons watching Dad navigate our boat through a potentially treacherous 500-foot span of the Delaware River, I was in the captain's chair.

I was terrified. I had thought I was prepared for this moment but navigating this stretch of water was proving to be far more complex than I had anticipated.

We were just north of the Dingman's Ferry Bridge, which connects New Jersey and Pennsylvania for the bargain fee of $1 per car. I had steered our boat close to a crumbling Native American crossing, built in the 1500s, that remains *in* the river. For my entire life, I have been told that the crossing was built by the Lenape tribe, but you will not find any mention of it in history books. It seems the crossing is only known to those of us who are adventurous enough to travel by boat north of the Dingman's Ferry Bridge. Or maybe, it's just Saia family folklore.

Either way, the crossing makes things difficult for boaters. There is precious little room for a boat to navigate. Each has to go through a narrow-fractured opening in the crossing without hitting either large rocks or being grounded in the shallow water on either side. Water rushes through, creating strong currents that work against boaters, pushing their vessels into the boulders they are desperately trying to avoid. The more it rains, the more dangerous it becomes inside the crossing's fracture.

All to say, a less-than-seasoned boater can have real difficulty staying on course. The unskilled get pushed into boulders that can flip even the most stable of boats.

The prize lies beyond the danger: some of the best fishing holes in the Delaware. I have many memories of my dad and me catching small mouth bass past the crossing. But let's get back to my first voyage at the helm.

Bang, screech, thump.

On that day in 1981, the sound of our boat hitting the boulders as the current pushed us into them stays with me. Dad's words offered a steady beat above the noise: "Stay left. Go slow. You got this kid."

We made it. I got through my first crossing without flipping the boat.

Years of watching and learning from my dad prepared me for the day I attempted to make the pass on my own. Even then I needed him there to guide me, offer words of encouragement and to catch me if I failed.

If you're reading this book, it's likely that you're beginning your own journey—and I don't mean on a river. I mean navigating the waters of your career. That's where I come in.

Throughout my life, whether steering a boat or making my way in the business world, I had the benefit of learning from others and my dad's steady hand and sage words. But in life, not everybody is gifted with that kind of awesome human instruction manual.

On the Delaware, my dad learned to become a great boating captain. He must have navigated the crossing a thousand times. Each time he did so, he got better and better. And he let me "learn on him".

I want to do the same for you as you begin your journey. My 30 years, rising to a CEO in a major global organization, counseling clients of all sizes, becoming an angel investor, working with regulators and becoming a board member at a major university, are filled with storms, treacherous currents and boulders of all sizes. "Learn on me". Consider this book your own personal GPS, showing you where you might want to stay left, hold steady or wait out a storm before proceeding.

Today, I have my own boat that leaves port from Southwick Marina in Long Beach Island, New Jersey. Many times, my sons are aboard with my wife and me. They are now the ones learning from me how to navigate the waters.

I share in this book with you as I do with them on the boat, through analogies and stories. I've chosen the animal kingdom for most of my chapters because in the business world, you'd be amazed at the similarities between humans and our wildlife counterparts. Sometimes that's funny, sometimes it's sad—but it's always interesting.

After each story, I'll give you some "Learn on me" words of advice as if we were in the boat together. That just felt right. It's how I grew up learning and believe it or not, some of the "old ways" still work better than anything else.

So, put on your lifejacket and bring your sense of humor and adventure.

Climb aboard. We have places to go.

You got this, kid!

PART 1: IT'S ABOUT YOU

The first section of this book is about you becoming your best self. Much of your career is about you, so we'll start there. In the second half of the book, we'll talk about how it's not all about you, though. Many strong individuals and forces will shape your career and you need to learn how to handle those situations.

But first, you.

A large portion of your success in life is dependent on you.

I witness so many people in the business world—of all ages and at all levels--forget personal responsibility. They blame others for their lack of success. They blame circumstances, like a market downfall, on their inability to effectively lead. And the most often used excuse of all, they complain about not having the time to focus on themselves.

If we could create perfect circumstances for everyone, we could all succeed. I could guarantee that you will be the next manager, division head, CEO or Chairman of the company of your choice. Maybe I could guarantee you that you will be the next head coach or General Manager of your favorite sports franchise. Or how about guaranteeing you that your startup will be sold for a billion dollars? Wouldn't that be nice?

Unfortunately, it's not that simple. Perfect circumstances rarely, if ever, occur. So, the wise thing to do is to work on what you *can* control—you.

In this section, we will focus on three simple stories from the animal world.

- Protect what makes you different. Mandarin ducks do.
- Butterflies are magnificent but they didn't start out that way.
- Developing a thick skin early will add years to your staying power. As you will see it works for armadillos.

Here we go.

MANDARIN DUCKS

YOUR X FACTOR IS YOUR SECRET SAUCE.
IT'S THE BEST THING YOU BRING TO THE
TABLE. BUT IT MAKES YOU A SITTING
DUCK.

DON'T LOSE YOUR SPECIAL SAUCE

In 2018, New York City was aflutter. The city's most eligible bachelor had arrived in the form of a Mandarin duck.

A duck that is normally not seen outside of east Asia. Mandarin ducks are quite beautiful—and especially so when swimming in a Central Park pond with ducks that look rather drab in comparison.

Blog posts, articles, news video, watercolor portraits—the city rushed to welcome the Mandarin duck.

But even as articles and social media went nuts for

Central Park's newest resident, the mystery of how he had ventured so far from his normal habitat remained. No one seemed to know where he came from. Even the Audubon.org editor, Andrew Del-Colle, chimed in, penning a letter to him:

> *Dear Duck Xiānshēng,*
>
> *. . . First off, I want to thank you. We don't know where you came from (someone's private collection maybe?) or why you suddenly appeared (you were crushingly lonely with no duck friends?), but you have captured the fascination of birders and non-birders alike, in New York City and around the world. That's no small thing. You've been featured by the New York Times, deemed the city's most eligible bachelor, and even got dubbed a "rock star" across the pond. You have a T-shirt now.*
>
> *There's no denying it: You are one hot duck."*

My young friends, as you enter the work world or begin a new leadership position, particularly if you have what are considered very hot, marketable skills, you will be like the Mandarin duck. Especially if your talents are immediately apparent and above those of some of your workmates. The red carpet will be rolled out and there may be a "buzz" about you. Everyone is checking out your mad skills to see for themselves.

And then Phase II begins.

But you also aren't that special, so don't go getting a big crest, okay? Yeah, you are exotic and unbelievably gorgeous with your dazzling plumage and majestic wing sails, but you're not quite the mysterious rarity that the Times and others first made you out to be. Vagrant Mandarin Ducks routinely pop up around the country. There's an established population in California. You aren't even a first for this city! So, sure, you're exciting and novel, but c'mon, it's us, we can be real here. Not to mention, your non-native garb is also showing up our most beautiful native duck. Don't think that Wood Duck doesn't mind. He does . . .

You'll be human. Not everyone will think you're a genius, like your ideas, appreciate your penchant for [fill-in-the-blank]. Whatever special sauce you bring, people will begin to poke holes.

Considering how popular you are, you probably have no idea that your appearance sparked some mixed reactions in the birding world, especially on Twitter (it's a communication platform where you can share these short messages called tweets with your followers and . . . nevermind). Reaction 1: A stunning duck that most people have never seen before and never will again—cool! Reaction 2: An exotic species that's clearly an escapee, doesn't count for your life list, and represents potential competition for endemics. . . . not that cool . . .

You will soon find out who your friends are—those that appreciate what you bring to the table—and who is observing your uniqueness as if you're a circus act. For entertainment purposes only. And they'll be critiquing from the cheap seats.

Maybe you bring a different voice or perspective from your company's cultural norm. Perhaps a bolder strategy or a new way of thinking. Possibly a work ethic like no other. But after the bloom is off the rose, you are vulnerable because of the very thing that attracted the company to you in the first place.

Central Park has been without its most eligible bachelor now since March 2019. That was the last time he was seen.

Theories abound, of course. Some say he was poached and eaten. Some say he met a nasty end by some unkind troublemakers or a hungry animal. Others offer that he may have flown to a smaller pond upstate and found himself quite happy there. Settled down, had a family.

No one really knows for sure. My guess is, he realized that what made him different attracted a lot of attention—and that can get old, even for a duck. I am hoping he took off to be "a big duck in a small pond" as they say.

As you enter new metaphorical ponds throughout your career, remember this little handsome guy. Protect what makes you different. Don't eliminate it, because it's what no one else can bring to the table. But find a pond that's friendly toward your unique attributes. One that not only allows you to spread your wings a bit, but one that makes you happy.

You came to this world to bring your own brand of special. Don't let the drab masses take that from you. Or squash you because of it. Be. Beautiful. You.

Let's go fishing: Learn on me

People who have worked with me have described me as a transformation agent, a pioneer, an independent thinker who looks at things differently. My leadership evaluations often include words like "creative, inspirational and authentic." This is part of my secret sauce. It makes me who I am. No one on this earth is like me. Just like no one on this earth is like you.

But let me save you the homework on secret sauces. I have two words for you that will save you a lot of time: They're subjective. One person's amazing roux is another's sour soup. Can you become an acquired taste for those who don't immediately appreciate you? Sure. I did, sometimes. But sometimes, no matter what you do, you just won't ever be someone's go-to choice.

As you read on you will learn that sometimes you need to adapt to survive. But that cannot be at the peril of your secret sauce. It is who you are. Compromise where you can, but not on your essence.

That means you need to decide what is "smart" for you in your career, rather than following one-size-fits-all career advice. One of my many coaches told me: "Chuck, your biggest asset is your creativity. Yet you have long to-do lists. Lose the to-do lists. It will liberate you and allow your creativity to flourish. Let yourself explode with ideas that could propel you and your teams to unimaginable positive outcomes." For me that changed everything. I was liberated!

As my career evolved, there are times I was asked to become different. Become more focused on the details. Tone down my energy. Play the political game more. Basically, become something that I am not. At those decision points, I had to choose.

I stayed true to my essence. If I had conformed more, I probably would have been given different opportunities. Some of those might have proved to be financially better for my family. But I knew the point past which I couldn't compromise. And if I had, it would have made me miserable and likely led to many failures.

If I had conformed, maybe I wouldn't have authored this book, served as a board member at a university, become an angel investor, enjoyed coaching my sons' little league baseball teams. Maybe if I had conformed more, I would have just taken my CPA certificate and given accounting advice. While there's no shame in that if it's your dream, that scenario makes my stomach hurt. I only chose to study accounting because my dad did. And it wasn't a good choice for someone with my sauce.

Like me, you will be given opportunities to be something you are not, or to be yourself. Choose to be you! It will make you happier in whatever pond you choose to swim.

BUTTERFLIES

BE WHO YOU ARE AND WHERE YOU ARE AT
EVERY STAGE OF YOUR CAREER. BUT
ADAPT. ALWAYS ADAPT.

STAY HUNGRY

Butterflies are the ultimate transformers. They reinvent themselves four times on their way to their final state, from an egg, to a caterpillar, to a chrysalis and finally, to a beautiful winged creature.

Only 10%, though, make it to the butterfly stage. But for those that do, the reward is great—flight.

Imagine an egg, a caterpillar, or a chrysalis trying to fly. Sounds ridiculous, right? But how many people do you see who try to run before they can walk? There's learning and growing to do at every stage. If you can embrace that learning and growing—even when it's not glamorous or the highest profile project or role at your organization—you'll go far in your career. Embracing every stage, from entry-level to young senior leader—and being humble enough to learn what you need to learn—will allow you to transform so you're ready for the next level.

Metamorphosis can only take place when you embrace where you are. Push too hard to skip stages of your career, and you're likely to miss key pieces of the transformation. Not accepting where you are—trying to jump ahead before you're ready--breeds inauthenticity. And that's dangerous. It puts you in the 90% that don't make it to real leadership.

Remember, you want to be in the 10% that fly. That means soaking in and digesting everything around you in order to grow. A caterpillar outgrows and sheds its skin up to five times and throughout its metamorphosis, consuming food so it can keep growing and changing.

When in chrysalis stage, our soon-to-be-butterfly still doesn't look (or probably feel) like a beautiful winged creature yet. From the outside, it looks as if progress and development has halted. But so much is going on in the inside. Similarly, at key points of your career, it may appear you're standing still. But you're not. If you're wise, you're taking courses, learning from more experienced professionals, taking stock of what your next career move should be. That's anything but standing still. Huge change is taking place—it's just on the inside, where it counts. No one else may see it, but it will help you immensely when you use your newfound knowledge and skills to make the leap to the next level, the next job, or even your next career.

When you finally hit your butterfly stage—whatever that looks like for you—all the hard work, decisions and changes you've made will pay off. You'll look back and be glad you embraced each stage of your metamorphosis. Trust me on this one.

. . .

Let's go fishing: Learn on me

Not every move in my career was "up." Some were horizontal, to gain a wider variety of experience. I would like to think I've never been arrogant about learning to build my knowledge as a leader.

Shortly after graduating with my MBA, I moved from a large aircraft manufacturing company to join one of the largest accounting and professional services firms in the world. Back then, everybody who graduated with an accounting degree wanted to work for one of the Big Eight Accounting Firms. I felt like I was taking my career in the right direction. I was still developing, with the promise of becoming a butterfly.

My first assignment was a staff auditor for one of our firm's best financial services clients. Boy was I excited. Of all the accounts I could have been assigned to, this was the Big Kahuna. I believed I was going to learn the financial markets firsthand by auditing one of the greatest financial institutions in the world. Fantastic!

On Day One, I received my orders. I was to go to the client's print shop in Somerset NJ. Then, I was supposed to watch workers print customer confirmations (an audit confirm is mailed to a customer to ensure the amount the client said the customer had on its books was what the customer had). I was instructed not to touch the confirmations - just to watch the workers print confirmations and mail them.

Within the first 20 minutes, I wanted to poke my eyes out. I felt like I was learning absolutely nothing. Zilch. Big zero.

On the second day my manager came to check on me. "How's it going?" he asked.

If I were on the playground in middle school, I probably

would have kicked his ass for asking me what appeared to be a really stupid question. Really? I thought I was going to learn the financial markets. Instead, I was watching people fix paper jams. How did he think it was going?

Luckily, I had left 1980's middle school logic behind. My real response was: "Great. I didn't realize how much it took to get these out. How hard these people work. I am seeing some inefficiencies that I have jotted down that I think could improve the process. I would like to share these with you when we are back at the office."

Inside, I wanted to complain. To tell him off for giving an MBA with previous experience a job babysitting print shop workers. But on my transformation journey, I was barely hatched. I needed to get through the stage I was in, proving myself, before I could fly with what I knew I was capable of.

My manager looked at me with disbelief. Not long after, he would later give me my next assignment, auditing derivatives. *Everyone* wanted to audit derivatives because they were the latest, hottest type of financial product on the market. I was being rewarded for my print shop efforts.

Remember me when your first assignment feels like watching paint dry. No matter how meaningless and boring you believe the task is, do it with as much gusto as you would if it were a plum assignment. Understand you are part of a bigger whole, a team. The energy you put forth will open doors for you.

That is how you get closer to flying.

ARMADILLO

THICK SKIN AND A SOFT HEART WILL TAKE YOU FAR.

FIND PEACE IN TURBULANT WATERS

In 2013, in Brazil, a Giant Armadillo named Alex was born to his mother, Isabelle. Many say Alex made incredible contributions to science, as researchers studied the sophisticated nurturing relationship baby armadillos have with their mothers by watching Alex with Isabelle.

Armadillos are the only living mammal with a hard shell. And a Giant Armadillo arguably has the thickest skin in the world. It's no surprise that "armadillo" is a Spanish word meaning "little armored one"—named for the bony plates that cover an armadillo's back, head, legs and tail. This thick protection helps keep an armadillo safe from predators who would attack its soft underbelly.

I am betting that you already know where I'm headed with this story, right? Anyone who has attended school for any length of time knows there are times when we all wish for some protective armor. From mean girls to schoolyard bullies, a little extra protection at times (for our softer side) sure would be nice.

I wish I could tell you the mean girls and bullies stay in the schoolyard but some of them follow you to the grownup playgrounds of corporate America. And poor Alex the Giant Armadillo succumbed to an attack by a bully in his world—a puma on the prowl.

In 2015, scientists spotted a vulture outside of Alex's den. When they dug up the burrow, they found Alex had died. He was just 23 months old (outlasting many CEO terms by at least five months—think about that). Unfortunately, his armor was not yet tough enough to withstand the puma attack. In a small victory, though, Alex managed to escape the puma's jaws and make it back to his burrow. Scientists believe he lasted another two days before the vultures started to gather.

You're not an armadillo. You are human, with a heart that can stay soft for all the right things and a brain that will tell you who is trustworthy, who is out to attack you, and everything in between. And you can begin to develop that wisdom long before you enter the business world.

Your thick skin will allow you to take in what is offered and weigh it before deciding what is valid and what is just an unwarranted attack. If you want to be a leader of any type, expect criticism and unsolicited opinions. When someone disagrees with you or attacks your ideas, your thick skin can make you a far more effective leader. Did you know that an armadillo can hold its breath for six minutes? Because they can do this, sometimes you will see them walk across the bottom of a clear river or stream, unperturbed by the turbulence in the water above them. So, in addition to thick skin—armadillos can remain in peaceful waters—getting through what would appear to be a difficult leg of their journey—because they can do something few land-based animals can. Channel your inner armadillo next time things get turbulent and you need to avoid being swept away by the current.

I'm not going to lie to you. Thick skin is usually developed on the job and the process is not, pleasant. You must be attacked or criticized to be able to see how thick yours is. Building that armor takes time and soul searching. You can't wall yourself in, but you can't be paralyzed because of what everyone else is saying either. You're great for a reason. Trust yourself.

Let's go fishing: Learn on me

I have a secret I turn to when I need to activate my thick skin while keeping my heart open. I think of that "thing" to which all else pales in comparison. Having survived the 9/11 terrorist attacks, that perspective comes more easily now than it did prior to 2001.

I was likely the last person from my organization inside of Two World Financial Center—I had to run the halls and make sure no one remained in their offices after the planes hit the buildings. All six floors. A lot of things run through your mind on a mission like that. My wife and kids. My wife and kids. I'll say it again—my wife and kids.

When I gave the all-clear, I walked outside to mayhem. The images etched in my mind--people jumping out of the upper floors—well, those never go away. When the first building went down, many of us headed south, which was the wrong direction because of the wind. As we watched in disbelief, a tidal wave of smoke and debris headed toward us as we ran from the first falling building to the end of the island, where the East River flows into the Hudson River. On a normal day, from this location the Staten Island Ferry leaves port from Manhattan. On that Tuesday, it was the backdrop of a scene I wouldn't have believed if I hadn't been living it.

I literally began to take my pants off in a crowd of hundreds of strangers. An avid outdoorsman, I knew I could make a raft out of them and was going to give it a try to escape what I saw heading toward us. Then someone yelled: "It's secondary smoke. You're going to be able to breathe." Thank God. We were sitting ducks otherwise.

At that point, I started running north. I couldn't reach my wife via my cell phone and I wanted to get to safety. I run marathons, so I figured if I just kept running, I could last for quite a while. If this sounds like a bad action flick, it felt that way also. Surreal. And not in a good way at all.

I was one of the lucky ones. I got to go home and live my life. But ever since then, promotions, making money, and all the rest of it just aren't important to me. Even today, I keep that perspective. Once you gain something that hard-earned, you don't lose it.

You'll have your own source of perspective. Maybe it's a parent or a grandparent. Maybe it's your faith or a desire to leave the world better than you found it. Everyone will have their own version. But find that thing. Identify it as such. And use it to remind yourself of what is truly important. It's like a turbo-boost to any necessary armored thick skin you've developed. But it will also ensure your heart stays open and where it needs to be—protected for those who need it most.

PART 2: IT'S NOT ALL ABOUT YOU

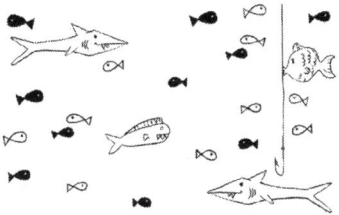

You can have the most special sauce, an uncanny ability to transform and the thickest skin in the world and still fail.

Why? Because it's about you, but not *all* about you.

That's a simpler phrase to read than it is to live. You need to work with the right mentors and teammates to make the right bets and to embrace diversity of thought that leads to success.

I got this right maybe 50% of the time. Even as I wrote this section, I found it hard not to go negative. I found myself wanting to share stories of the people I would like to blame for my shortcomings. For my failures. But I own my career and made my own choices. Just like you will.

Hopefully you'll do better than my 50% success rate in this area. Remembering what I share in this section should help you:

- Stay away from scorpions. They're career ruiners.
- Find yourself a pod of dolphins. They'll help in stormy seas.
- Just like a wise eagle, feed your team equitably.
- Embrace diversity. Every puppy has a unique quality.

SCORPIONS

RECOGNIZE A HOSTILE WORK
ENVIRONMENT. AND MOVE ON—AS
QUICKLY AS YOU CAN—TO A NURTURING
ONE.

Choose your pack leader carefully, my young friends.

This is not just to help your career. It's for survival.

For example, scorpions are known to be among the least kind creatures of the animal kingdom, making liberal use of deadly venom. Not only will they kill predators, they'll also kill some of their weaker young to survive. Cannibalism among scorpions of the same species is so common that young scorpions often instinctively feed and travel at different times than their elders—just to avoid being eaten. They learn young how to survive.

They're wise to be cautious. Full-grown scorpions are tough little beasts, the world's oldest surviving animal. They can survive long periods in freezing temperatures or in the blistering heat of 115 degrees Fahrenheit. They can withstand heavy doses of radiation. They've been found living in caves a half mile below the earth's surface, and under snow-covered rocks 14,000 feet up in the Himalayas. To say they're seasoned is an understatement.

The corporate equivalent of scorpions are managers or team leaders who will throw your reputation or career path away to save their own. They, too, are "tough little beasts." When an emergency project comes along—as they often do—with too few resources and not enough time for successful completion, a scorpion manager will throw it your way and then head home for dinner. After all, you're the new kid on the block, the work horse. They won't care if you're up through the night trying to get it done. They don't offer you resources. They just want you to make them look good.

If, by some miracle, that happens, you'll survive to do it all over again when the next emergency hits. Lucky you. And if you don't pull it off, your name is the one thrown around for subpar performance. Scorpion toxin is a powerful nerve poison, which explains why victims often feel like they have been jolted by an electric shock when they get stung. And that's probably how you will feel the first time you experience a human scorpion figuratively throwing you under the bus.

Describing death from a scorpion sting, the zoologist J.L. Cloudsley-Thompson wrote, "First, a feeling of tightness develops in the throat so that the victim tries to clear his throat of an imaginary phlegm . . . The victim next becomes restless and there may be slight, involuntary twitching of the muscles . . . Convulsions follow, the arms are flailed about and the extremities become quite blue before death occurs." Sound horrific? It is. I've seen a metaphorical version of this happen in conference rooms where a junior team member realizes they've just been "stung" by their team leader. It's never pretty.

Remember: a scorpion manager will not stand shoulder to shoulder with you. But they're happy to take credit when you pull off an amazing feat.

The good news is, you can identify scorpions if you pay attention. They're easy to spot—all you have to do is be alert. My advice: find another animal den, aka team, to join. Find a mother bear who would die to feed and protect you. One who will ensure you're not left behind. You'll never change a scorpion's behavior, so use your energy to instead move yourself out of stinging range. Could you stay and try to work through the situation? Sure. And some leaders will tell you that builds character. I feel it wastes time. You are going to do great things, right? So put your energy into those, positively, rather than fighting a negative manager.

Let's go fishing: Learn on me

I chose many mentors and colleagues who were not like scorpions. Each took an interest in my success. They were mother bears who took time to coach me, provide advice and or to simply care about my career and well-being. Today many of these individuals have retired or are approaching retirement but they remain my mentors.

That is not to say that I didn't experience many scorpions along the way. Plenty of people stole my ideas without offering credit, quietly said less than stellar things about me behind my back and took pleasure in taking me and others down. I don't mean to paint a negative picture—there are plenty of great people along the way—but as you start out, you must be realistic. Many people are attracted to business because they have an ego to feed, rather than because they want to innovate. The scars I have from those people are one of the reasons I chose to write this book--to help you avoid them.

Here's a story that illustrates what a good manager and mentor does. At a certain point in my career, my manager was skyrocketing into leadership. He was doing so with the help of my work. I was ok with that, because he always positioned me well, generously making sure I had exposure to firm leaders and key clients so I could show them my worth. He was happy when I succeeded.

One day, I received a call from the executive suite upstairs. Two of our top leaders wanted to speak to me. One would eventually become our CEO, the other a highly successful Senior Partner. Both went on to sit on various Corporate Boards. In that meeting they asked me to be their Chief of Staff.

Taking the role meant my career would take off. I was eight years into the professional ranks, and this was my opportunity to leapfrog to the next level. I was torn because I knew leaving my manager would hurt him. But he put that aside to encourage me in my career, saying, "Chuck, this is a no-brainer. Do it."

A scorpion he was not. My time with him and them changed the trajectory of my career. Find your equivalent by choosing your mentors wisely.

DOLPHINS

NOBODY IS AN ISLAND. AT LEAST NOT HAPPILY OR SUCCESSFULLY.

November 8 (my birthday by the way), 2007 in California, a great white shark attacked a surfer who had been enjoying some gnarly waves. During the attack, a pod of dolphins rushed in to form a ring around him to ensure the shark couldn't go in for a second strike. Eventually, their efforts drove the shark off and the surfer was brought to the safety of shore.

A different day in New Zealand, four swimmers—one a lifeguard--were saved from an almost 9-foot long great white shark by a group of dolphins who encircled them for safety. When one tried to escape the circle, unaware of what was happening, two of the larger dolphins herded him back quickly.

Dolphins rock.

Talk about a happy mammal. Dolphins are social animals who use pulsating sounds and pure tones to communicate. And communicate they do, within their pods and in larger groups (herds) when pods join to hunt or defend against predators.

Scientists remain unsure if it's this communication, a natural predilection for group cooperation or a combination of factors—but dolphins clearly are natural teamers. When a member is injured, they will physically support it to take it to the surface so it can breathe through its blowhole. When hunting large schools of fish, dolphins' team and take turns so all can feed.

And, just like humans tend to have multiple team situations during their career, dolphins will likely have multiple pods throughout their lifetimes. They'll move on for a variety of reasons, but generally team no matter what pod they land in.

Offer dolphins a reward, and they'll up their teaming game (also a bit like humans). At the Dolphin Research Center in the Florida Keys, researchers had dolphins swim across a lagoon at different times. But they had to press a button at the same time. If they did, they received fish and praise—two things dolphins really love.

Researchers found that the dolphins' behavior changed as they repeated the task. Even though they were signaled to swim at different times, the dolphins eventually learned to wait to press their respective buttons within .37 of a second. I can assure you, having worked with humans for many years, we are too often not as smart as dolphins when it comes to teaming. I've been on teams where rewards for cooperation and group wins were at the ready, but the team couldn't pull together and tamp down egos enough to be a real team.

On the flip side, I've worked with some people and produced an end result exponentially better than any of us could have done on our own. The difference? You have to value the common good, not just your own advantage. A good team helps a member who is struggling, combines efforts toward a collective goal, bands together and disbands with goodwill. And throughout it all, they communicate to keep everyone focused, safe and moving in the right direction.

Don't be the person who acts as an island. Even if you're an introvert who would rather work alone. Even if teaming is hard for you. In any organization, you need allies. You need people who help you not only perform your best, but also be your best. Sometimes that's challenging. But people are part of the equation. Learning how to team well with them will do more for your career than just about anything else. I speak from experience.

Let's go fishing: Learn on me

Things were good for me a decade into my career. I was skyrocketing. Yes, actually being told the sky is the limit, but I still had a lot to learn.

An athlete my whole life, growing up I was on various baseball, basketball and football teams. I pitched in championship games, played point guard in playoffs and despite my small stature, even captained our football team in high school. I thought I knew teaming. But the business world threw me some curveballs.

A dozen or so years into my professional life, I would learn the value of teaming like never before when I was assigned a project with another young partner. She had a reputation for being a hard worker, smart, articulate and creative. I barely knew her at the time. We were asked to develop a strategy for a new business.

We had four weeks to prepare and present a proposed strategy to not just any committee, but one that had a reputation for being made up of real sharks. I believe we were the third team asked to present a strategy. The first two lost limbs. I was afraid we'd be eaten alive.

Week One into developing the strategy, my partner was quiet. Or maybe the young me was verbose, had all the answers and didn't value her ideas. I was polite, asked for input, but I was often too "large and in charge," talking over her, bulldozing over her quiet demeanor.

We were getting nowhere. Or rather, I was getting nowhere sitting on an island all by myself. My vision of us being eaten alive seemed very likely.

In Week Three, we had a moment that we still talk about today. In it, I learned the true value of teaming and she learned she had a voice. It changed the outcome of our presentation and frankly, our careers. As we discussed the strategy we were going to present, I lead or, better said, controlled the dialogue. Because of course I, the great Chuck Saia, needed to make sure this didn't go off the rails. Then, at one of our daily meetings, everything shifted.

While I preached the merits of yet another of my ideas as we discussed direction for our presentation, out of nowhere she launched into her own idea. She spoke with conviction, with confidence and passion.

Who was this person? She was awesome! After she pitched it to me, she asked what I thought. I said, "Ok." It was a plain ok, without a lot of enthusiasm. She then asked, "Chuck - do you really mean ok? Are you really in?" I said, "You sounded so confident and sure about this that I'm sure you're right and I'm ready to go all in on it."

Her idea really was fantastic. From that point on, we teamed more as equals who respected what each brought to the table—recognizing we had different perspectives, which was our strength.

But the learning was not done.

Something didn't occur to me during our preparation. Because we didn't really know each other and swam in different circles, she had different allies on the executive committee than I did. This would prove advantageous for both of us.

That realization didn't occur to me until, during our presentation, a shark she knew very well attacked me. Like a dolphin teaming, she swooped in and chased him away, validating my idea. I reciprocated immediately when a shark attacked her, launching in to protect her and her idea. It easily could have been a feeding frenzy, but it wasn't. Do you know why?

As a team we presented. As a team we defended. As a team we swam through the sharks with ease, selling our strategy. And they bought it. They all bought it. No limbs lost.

Years later, she invited me to a women-in-leadership forum to speak. As she introduced me, she told this story and how it changed her. She thanked me. I was flattered and still am. But until this writing I didn't realize how much it changed me.

With that, I say thank you to my fellow dolphin pod mate. It took me far too long. Don't make that mistake.

EAGLES

AN INSPIRATIONAL LEADER SEES BEYOND THE SQUEAKY WHEEL.

EVERY BIRD GETS THE WORM

Imagine, early spring in Alaska, two eagles—a male and a female—begin building a nest. They gather twigs and brush to create a sturdy home for the eaglets that would hatch in a little over a month. In the eagle world, as in our human world, location is everything. With a bird's eye view of the nearby mountains and water, the nest was the equivalent of every new parent's wish list—a house with good bones, in a neighborhood with good schools.

The pair tended to the nest, protecting the eggs until eaglets emerged. And what happens next will not surprise those of you with brothers or sisters or zoologists—sibling rivalry began. Wildlife observers have found at its worst, larger eaglets will outmaneuver smaller ones for the morsels of food brought back to the nest. It is sometimes a case of the louder, more persistent eaglet—the "squeaky wheel"—gets more food and more attention.

But not in this nest. Every time the mama eagle brought food back to the nest from the nearby river or mountain, she made sure food was distributed equally. She saw promise in both of her chicks, as different as they were. She also knew both could thrive in the wild if only she fed them, encouraged them and gave them an equal start in life.

Later that year, this eagle mother sat proudly on her perch, watching both of her children soar through the Alaskan sky. Her work was done.

I wish I could see every corporate equivalent of this story end so beautifully. As you progress through the ranks, it's likely you'll manage a team of people if you are not already doing so. Let me assure you, in case you have any doubt—there is always a squeaky wheel. There's always at least one person on your team who uses some form of superiority as an advantage—experience, key relationships, connections outside of work. And sometimes, gender or race. It's sad but true.

Regardless of the specifics of the team you will one day lead, please remember this eagle mom. Everyone has potential. A truly inspirational leader "feeds" his or her team equitably so all have an equal chance of reaching their personal potential. Will all fly at the same height? Probably not. But each should be able to achieve to the best of their ability. That's success.

The squeaky wheel is not necessarily the team member that is the most deserving or has the most potential. Sometimes your most reticent employee is full of great promise and you have to draw it out. I've never been sorry for biasing toward "equal inspiration" and following it up with equal coaching, resources and time with the boss (me).

Let's go fishing: Learn on me

This section may be my favorite of all. I believe a true leader understands the value of feeding all their eaglets. Time and time again I have witnessed areas of the business getting the most resources simply because they're the biggest, initiatives getting the most attention because they solve immediate problems ("short-term think" is terrible for business), or worst of all, people being promoted simply because they look and act exactly like the leader promoting them. The result is a lot of starved eaglets and the eventual extinction of anyone or anything other than mainstream.

Eventually this lack of distributed feeding not only kills diverse thought, it leads to a company's extinction. Think about all the retailers who could have become the next online superstore. If you don't think somewhere someone at a bookstore chain or retailer HQ said in meetings, "We need to aggressively invest in online operations and shift our business from brick and mortar," you're fooling yourself.

My biggest pleasure has been feeding people and watching them grow. I've enjoyed this even more than seeding lucrative new businesses. Nothing beats helping a fellow human evolve and reach lofty goals. I mean it.

How do you feed a person in the business world? Through support and mentorship. Both require a leader's precious time. However, it's time well spent.

Today I am mentoring many professionals while I enjoy watching those I've mentored in the past grow into eagles. I am careful about who I mentor. I need to be able to offer something and they need to be willing to listen. You can't feed an eagle who doesn't want to eat.

As I write this, I am beaming with pride as I think about

all the people who have allowed me to be a part of their career journey. For instance, a young partner I met while she was helping my team drive a strategic initiative comes to mind. Though she appeared quiet at the time, when she spoke, she came across as smart, articulate and disarming-an impressive feat! I thought to myself at the time: she is a hidden gem.

Five short years later, as CEO, I offered her a job as my CFO. She was not the obvious choice, but I knew she would shine, given the right opportunity. The offer surprised her because she never imagined herself in that role and wasn't sure others would see her as a fit. When I explained I put her there because I wanted her to stretch outside of her comfort zone, to help her learn new skills and strengthen more muscles, she began to understand. While many others were asking for the opportunity, I gave someone who was not the squeaky wheel a chance. I was right about her from the start.

The world has changed since then. Today, more often than not, I am asked directly to be a mentor. Recently a rising executive, who wants to be the CEO of a technology company, approached me to mentor him. Though we only met briefly, once, he mustered up the courage to ask me. He was unaware that at our first meeting I was already sizing him up. I thought to myself: another hidden gem. Of course, I would mentor him.

Each time we meet, he thanks me for my mentorship, the advice I give him, the contacts I have provided. While I appreciate the thanks, a true leader loves to coach. I sometimes feel I should be thanking him.

Remember that when you're in your new nest. Ask to be fed. You will grow because of it.

DOGS

THE MUTT MODEL: DIVERSITY OF THOUGHT, TRAITS, AND BACKGROUND BRINGS BALANCE

BREED DIVERSITY

A purebred German Shepherd is a gorgeous dog. Originally bred for herding sheep, it runs fast and pivots on a dime. Combine that with strength and natural intelligence and you have a stellar animal. It's no surprise these dogs help our military in critical situations.

While valued for their strengths, some purebred German Shepherds have begun to suffer because they've been bred exclusively so humans can harness those strengths. From hip dysplasia, to osteoarthritis, to hemophilia, this breed is now at risk of not being able to do what it's always done best.

Because too much of a good thing is never a good thing. Over-breeding is creating some sad realities throughout the dog kingdom.

I want you to think of human teams at work. The evidence shows that diversity makes a company more profitable and more innovative—not by a small margin, but by leaps and bounds. Diversity of gender, of race and ethnicity —but also diversity of thought and experience. The more perspectives and rich history people bring to the conference table or virtual brainstorm, the better the solutions and service they provide. In this manner, companies avoid blind spots. They avoid over-indexing on any one "good" brand attribute or activity because they see that—just like the dog kingdom—too much of a good thing is never a good thing.

Am I saying that the best organizations resemble a mutt more than a purebred because of the diversity of talents, thought and approaches? Yes. But I wouldn't recommend using the mutt analogy with your CEO. Wink, wink. Just a hunch.

Let's go fishing: Learn on me

In first grade, my friend Walter absolutely blazed in gym class each week. He was faster than any other classmate, the only one that could beat me in a footrace. I had him in stickball, though; I could hit better.

At that young age, athletics was about the only thing I cared about, so of course Walter and I became friends.

For weeks, I would talk about Walter at the dinner table. "Mom, he is FAST! Dad, he is so athletic. You will love Walter."

What I didn't say: Walter was Black. Because in first grade, thankfully I hadn't yet been taught by American culture to see the color of someone's skin as something that mattered.

One day, my mom allowed me to have a play date. I was so excited to bring Walter home from school with me. And that is the day I learned about racism.

My mom is one of the most progressive, spiritual and eclectic women I know. She has always been a staunch advocate for women's rights. A former Catholic turned Buddhist, she has infused every conversation with wise, loving thoughts into just about every conversation I have had with her since I was a young child. She would preach: "Love all God's creatures," or "Be in the present moment."

True to her beliefs, mom filled with pride that I didn't see color. That when I brought Walter home, he was just the fastest boy in the class, rather than anything else. She told the story over and over again—how proud she was that I brought a Black friend home without realizing he was Black. And while that likely had a positive effect in reinforcing how important it is to "love all of God's creatures," Mom was proving to be like most adults I knew in the 1970s--everyone saw color. Even mom. I just hadn't realized it until then.

Walter and my mom's reaction to him had a significant impact on me. But it wasn't until I was much older that I was able to translate that impact into something bigger—change I could help create. The biggest impact on me in my professional life is the day I took part in an inclusion training on unconscious bias.

Before that day, I thought I knew what made a good team. But on that day, I realized that diversity of thought is the most powerful thing a team can have. But it's not as simple as just pulling together a diverse team based on race, gender, or a host of other traits. I learned that a diverse team also needs to explore unconscious biases to truly succeed. It can be challenging, but it makes any team stronger. We did that one day at an offsite meeting with an organization I am a part of. The beautiful horse farm setting, replete with running trail and fishing ponds, seemed a perfect place to let our minds run wild with a renewed focus on team diversity.

In that bucolic setting, though, we were asked for some tough work. The leader-initiated conversations about biased behavior. Each of us shared stories about either witnessing, being a target of, or an actor of biased behavior. Talk about vulnerability.

To this day, I still remember every story told.

I watched a brilliant, diverse woman, whose career has involved working at various companies and government agencies all over the world, explain that a leader once told her she had three strikes against her because she was African American, Christian and a woman. She explained this wasn't the first-time racism and bias thought attacked who she was. She is a fighter and still managed to make it to the highest levels of corporate America and within the government agencies she has worked. While she told her story, I marveled at her seeming ability to brush off the bias. To this day, I still marvel at her ability to bring her own brand of different thinking to every conversation.

The stories kept rolling in . . .

I watched another woman struggle as she told the story of the bias, she experienced growing up a woman in Europe's male-dominated culture.

Another team member wept as he explained that he witnessed a person of short stature on his team become a victim of bias when a client said, "we don't want to be the tallest midget in our industry." He regrets he did nothing to console her. She has since passed away, making his heart hurt more because he never addressed it with her at the time.

Finally, I relayed a story of watching my son on the pitching mound against his high school's archrival. As he pitched, kids on the other team threw antisemitic slurs at him because of his Jewish background (my wife is Jewish). He powered through it. I was proud of him, but it was hard to watch.

There were more stories and despite how different they were, we found commonality in our experience of bias. We came to better understand our differences in a more intimate way. This made us stronger as a team. There were no pedigrees among us. We were not manager or employee, straight or gay, Black or Asian. We were just human beings, all of whom had experienced the pain bias or prejudice brings.

The power of diversity is so simple. Over the years, having diverse teams not only protected us from my personal shortcomings, it also enriched our teams because of the variety of perspectives and good ideas brought to the table.

I am Italian American, half Sicilian. A Jersey Italian American, different than my counterparts in Staten Island, Philly, etc. My father is Catholic. My mother is Buddhist. My wife is Jewish. If all my teams had the same make-up as me, they would have been the weaker for it. Not because there is anything wrong with who I am or where I come from. But because our similarity of thought would have kept us from some great discoveries and outcomes. And a bunch of me's would have gotten contentious at some point, likely dislodging something—a hip, a knee—you name it. The hip injury would have shortened my career, making me unable to run nearly as fast as Walter.

Yes, I'm joking. But not about my larger point: in our differences lie our strengths.

CONCLUSION: THE WORLD
NEEDS YOU

The climate in which you are building a career today is worlds away from the one I joined years ago.

But one thing remains the same at its core: our basic humanity. People are people—always have been and always will be. You can see the same triumphs and dramas playing out through the ages.

So, as you witness agile startups that are changing entire industries and watch large, established organizations struggle to transform themselves to keep up, remember one thing: You're here for a reason.

You've been placed wherever you are at this very moment in time for a reason you may not even have begun to fathom. Or maybe you've known the reason for years now. Either way, I wrote this book to help encourage you the way my father encouraged me that day on the river.

You may be entering the workforce or a leadership position while dealing with a turbulent economy, lost jobs, a global pandemic, an uncertain future because of things like global warming, a civil movement, and more. But your generation brings a wisdom mine didn't. You're merging business and values, social responsibility and profits. It's long overdue and not an easy task.

But, YOU GOT THIS KID!

Like our friend the duck, you'll protect your "secret sauce-" that thing you bring to the table that no one else can. You'll toughen up your skin like the armadillo, just enough to withstand attacks from those who don't appreciate your uniqueness. And you'll transform into better and better versions of yourself as you go, thanks to lessons from our friend, the butterfly.

You got this, kid, because you also know it's not all about you.

You know to stay away from scorpions. Instead, you will follow mentors and leaders who want you to succeed. You will team like a dolphin because you know that your own strengths, merged with those of your colleagues; make fending off sharks much easier.

You appreciate that all eagles can fly and that the best leaders nurture all their chicks, not just the ones who chirp the loudest. Finally, you understand that too much of any one thing is not a good thing. Just like in man's best friend, the dog, diversity is healthy for companies and teams.

But most of all, you got this because you're the kind of person wise and motivated enough to read a book like this one. Which tells me a lot about you. Keep that spirit and drive.

The world could sure use you right about now.

ACKNOWLEDGMENTS

I have many people to thank, including friends, colleagues and family members. I could not have done this without your encouragement from start to finish. I am truly blessed to have so many incredible people in my life. Thank you!

With specific acknowledgement;

To the students; Amy Burstin, Quinnipiac University M.A. '21, Olamide Gbotosho, B.S. Quinnipiac University '21, Alexia Papavasilakis, B.S. Parsons School of Design, The New School '21, who helped get *You Got This, Kid! Worlds of Advice for Young Leaders* through the crossing without it hitting any "boat flipping" boulders, thank you!

To those that helped shape my voice and edit the book, thank you!

Finally, to those of you who purchased the book in order to have a positive impact on Lupus and Environmental Sustainability Studies, thank you.

WHY ENVIRONMENTAL SUSTAINABILITY AND LUPUS

An avid fisherman, Chuck Saia can be found fishing lakes, ponds, streams, rivers and oceans in Southern New Jersey. His love of the sport and desire for cleaner and healthier fisheries compelled him to donate half the proceeds of the book to environmental sustainability studies.

Lupus is a disease that devastates individuals and their families. Lupus has impacted the Saia family significantly, which is why the other half of the book's proceeds is allocated to Lupus research.

The Saia family established the Saia Family Fund at Quinnipiac University where all proceeds of this book will be directed for these two causes. It should be proudly noted that Chuck Saia is a member of Quinnipiac University's Board of Trustees and chairs its Futures Committee.

Made in the USA
Middletown, DE
18 October 2022